FOOTSTEPS IN THE WALLS AND OTHER MYSTERIES

CHARLOTTE EVELYN SLOAN

Footsteps in the Walls and other Mysteries

Copyright © 2021 by Charlotte Evelyn Sloan

All rights reserved. No part of this book may be reproduced or transmitted in any form by any means, electronic or mechanical, including photocopying and recording, or by any information storage and retrieval system, without permission in writing from the publisher, Marmie's Corner.

ISBN   978-1-7775187-8-3 (Paperback)
ISBN   978-1-7775187-9-0 (EPUB)

Are you a detective?

Look at the picture on the cover of this book. I spied that buffalo skull last spring in the shallow water at the edge of a lake and took a picture. When I saw it, I had some questions. Why was it there? How did that beast die and when? (By the way, there is an unplanned, hidden picture in that photograph. Can you find it?)

When you see something unusual, do questions buzz around in your head? Do you wonder what happened? Are you curious as a cat? This book contains several mystery stories that will make you think. I wonder which one will be your favorite.

Contents

Are you a detective? 3
Dragonflies in Taiwan 7
The Light in Grandpa Billy's Car 9
A Baby for Katie Holmes – Story 1 12
A Baby for Katie Homes - Story 2 14
A Tuk-tuk Just in Time 15
A Baby Crying in the Night 18
Ocean on the Prairie 20
Black Angel 21
Footsteps in the Wall 23
Ned Walker's Horses 27
The Dying Chickens 31
A Fur Coat in July 35
A Plumeria Blossom 37
Toddler in the Wheat Field 39
Treasure in the Cellar 41
Wait Here! 44
Fog on the River 45
When Lassie Hid the Pups 47
Who Said That? 50
Take Me Home! 52
High and Lifted Up 55
A Wet Night on the Highway 57
Donkey Come Home 60
Farewell Note 63

Dragonflies in Taiwan

This afternoon we noticed the air suddenly fill with hundreds and hundreds of dragonflies. Where did they come from, and why are there so many of them?

I am visiting the beautiful island of Taiwan. For several days the weather forecasters on radio and TV have been warning of a strong typhoon headed this way. I wonder if the dragonflies always show up before a typhoon. Maybe the heavy winds bring them across the water. I am confident that there must be an explanation in the wonderful world of nature.

CHARLOTTE EVELYN SLOAN

Strange and unusual events happen somewhere on the earth every day. No doubt there is almost always a logical explanation. Sometimes the mystery is easily solved, but other times we are left to ponder the reasons why.

The Light in Grandpa Billy's Car

Grandpa Billy and Baby Shelley

We always knew when my Grandpa arrived because he'd drive into our yard, stop the car, roar it as loud as possible and then turn off the engine. After he was gone, we missed his daily visits.

Grandpa Billy died in September. He was old and he had a bad heart but some people think he could have lasted a lot longer if they hadn't taken away his car. Actually, they didn't. He still owned his old blue Mercury, but after he and another old man in town had a fender bender, the police confiscated both of their driver's licenses.

It broke my Grandpa's heart not to be able to drive any more. I suppose if he had been able to pass a driver's test, they likely would have issued him another license but at age 81, he likely wouldn't have been successful.

One cold fall evening in October, about one month after Billy died, my Mom came in from outside with a puzzled look.

"I know this is crazy, but there's a light out in Dad's car." Of course we all trooped outside with her, and my Dad offered to investigate. Sure enough, as we stood there shivering together, keeping our distance, we all could clearly see an eerie, bluish light inside the old car. The light was pretty well exactly where the driver's head would be when driving.

By the light of the moon we watched my Dad approach the vehicle. He opened the car door, bent down and looked inside.

"Now it's gone!" he called out to us.

"No it's not, Dad. It's still shining!" He checked the other side of the car and opened that door, too.

"Looks like seeing the light depends on where I'm standing," said my Dad, who was determined to figure it out. Soon he crossed the yard to where we were waiting.

"It's only the moon," he said. "It's shining on the rear view mirror and reflecting the light on to the car seat."

The excitement was over. I looked over my shoulder. The pale blue light was still there. Strange happenings often have a practical solution. We hurried back into the warm house. I was glad my Dad had solved the mystery of the light in Grandpa Billy's car.

A Baby for Katie Holmes – Story 1

This story happened in the "pioneer days" when the province of Saskatchewan was welcoming new settlers. People came from around the world. For only $10 a homesteader could realize the dream of owning land. Katie and Billie Holmes were two of these immigrants. By their second summer in Canada, they were well established and had a reputation of being good neighbours to the hundreds of settlers moving in each week. The kettle was always on the stove in Katie Holmes' cheery kitchen. A knock on the door was never a surprise.

On a late summer afternoon, a young woman holding a baby appeared on the other side of the kitchen screen door.

Without introducing herself, she told Katie she was on her way to town and had a favor to ask.

"May I leave my baby with you? He's too heavy to carry any further."

Katie was from Nebraska. She was known all around the country side for the way she talked.

"You sure can, honey. You jes-a leave that lil' one here with me and go do whatever you got to do in town."

The girl seemed to be in a hurry. She walked out the lane and down the road towards town. Katie had no children of her own but she was well experienced, even offering her home as a place for women to come when it was time to deliver their babies. She set about heating milk for the baby, expecting to keep him only for the afternoon.

By nightfall the baby's mother had not returned. The next day Katie sent Billie by horse and buggy to ask the neighbours if they had seen her. He drove on into town to see if she was lost and perhaps trying to find her way back to their farm.

As it turned out, the girl was never seen again. It is supposed she caught the evening train and traveled on to some other location to start a new life in the 'wild west'. She had said the baby was too heavy to carry any further. Perhaps her words had a deeper meaning. The responsibility of the baby may have been too much of a burden for her at that time.

This mystery was never solved. Katie named the baby "Oscar"… and she 'jes-a' loved him all his life, as if he was he was her own!

A Baby for Katie Homes - Story 2

A friend of mine heard a totally different story about how Katie Holmes got her baby. She was told that Katie always wanted to become a mother but sadly, that didn't happen. One day she heard some very exciting news. Apparently, there was a little orphan baby 'up north', many miles away, who needed a home. Katie decided she'd take him, sight unseen!

She packed a lunch, hitched up their horse to the buggy and called to her husband, Billy. "I'm headin' out to get us a baby. You jes-a keep the house warm for when we get home! " Late that night Katie and little Oscar were welcomed home. Billy had a good warm fire in the kitchen stove, and he had milk and baby bottles waiting.

So now we have another mystery—which story is the truth? I honestly don't know but when I was young girl, I did meet Oscar Holmes. Of course he was grown up by then and had a pretty wife and some kids and he bragged that his waist measured 60 inches around!

A Tuk-tuk Just in Time

I know a young woman who moved to Guatemala to teach school. She didn't know anyone who lived there, she didn't have a house to live in and she couldn't understand or speak Spanish. She had obtained a job through the internet, and flew down there in July so she would be ready for school starting at the end of August. A staff member from the school was supposed to meet her when they arrived, and help her find a house, but that person didn't show up.

The woman and her six year old son stayed in a hotel for more than a week. Every day they went around town and tried to find a place to live. Most of the people spoke only Spanish and it seemed there were very few places available 'se renta'. It was lonely and extremely hard to settle in to their new town.

Finally, some good news! A storekeeper helped them find a house to rent. The landlord put in a stove and fridge. They bought food and dishes in the local market and little by little, they managed to make their house a home. Part of the house was a closed in garden where they hung beautiful flowering plants and washed their clothes by hand on an outdoor washstand, pronounced "pela' in Spanish. They needed other furniture and supplies. The teacher hired a carpenter to make a table and two chairs.

When the work was done and she went to pay him, the carpenter insisted on charging much more than they had agreed upon in the first place. It was hard to insist on her rights when she couldn't speak the language. So, even though she was discouraged, she paid the man and carried the chairs through town to her home. She asked around about a truck or some way to move the table. No help was available. She carried the table out on to the street, thinking she'd have to haul it home on her back. It was too heavy. She sat down on the curb and her little son sat beside her. It had been a long ten days of frustration, right from the moment they landed at Guatemala City airport.

Sitting there on the sidewalk, she said two words that she may never had said before—"I quit!" At that moment, she felt like they were at the end of the road. Just then, a young man pedaling a three wheel bike stopped in front of her. Built onto the back of the bike was a wide seat for passengers. That's how he made his money-- giving people taxi or "tuk-tuk" rides around town.

"I can fit your table on here," he said in cheerful English. The young woman and her boy trotted along beside the driver as he pedaled to their house and unloaded the table. She paid him and said how glad she was that he had come to the rescue. "I was ready to give up."

"Oh, don't ever give up!" he said, smiling, as he pointed to the hand-painted sign on the front of his tuk-tuk. It was one word: "Angel." (Here is the table transported by the tuk-tuk.)

FOOTSTEPS IN THE WALLS AND OTHER MYSTERIES

A Baby Crying in the Night

Carrie was a young mother with two babies of her own. On a cold fall night, she hurried outside to grab a few sticks of firewood. That's when she heard it--the sound of a tiny baby crying. It came from the trees that edged their yard. Carrie dropped the firewood and ran toward the sound. She stopped and heard it again, perhaps a little further away than she had first thought. By the sound of the crying, the young mom could tell it was a very young baby who must have been abandoned in the woods.

She began to run toward the sound, and then went further and further into the trees. The crying continued. Carrie was certain she would find the baby any minute. Each time she thought she was almost there, the sound was just a little further away. Eventually, she found herself deep in the dark woods, alone, more than half a mile from her house. She faced the realization that the 'baby' she heard crying could not possibly have moved that far or that fast.

"Carrie!" She was relieved to hear her husband call her name and in a few minutes he was there beside her. She started to cry, telling him about the sound of the baby out here in the dark, and how quickly it had moved. He put his arm around her, and as they walked back to the house, he explained. "That's no baby, but it certainly does sound like one. Actually, it's a wild animal that I have seen and heard before." Just then, they heard the sound again, but this time it was faint and far away.

Carrie shivered." What does it look like?" she asked.

Her husband answered, "It looks like a very big cat. Don't worry, Carrie, you are not the first or the last person to be fooled by the sound of a lynx!"

Ocean on the Prairie

When I was a child I always wanted to see the ocean. One day my mother said to me, "If you are lucky, some day you will see the ocean on the prairie." When I asked her what she meant, she told me that when the wheat is ripe and golden and waving in the breeze and the hot summer sun is shining in just the right way, I might see what looks for all the world like the shimmering water of a huge lake. I doubted that I would ever be so fortunate as to see it.

But I did! On very hot day in August I was riding in my Uncle Hec's old blue truck. We were going for a drive to see if his fields were ready for harvest. As we topped a hill with miles of wheat fields to the west of us, he suddenly stopped the truck. We got out and he pointed, not saying a word. All I could see was sparkling water, as huge as the ocean.

A wheat field looks like the ocean only on a very hot day when weather conditions are perfect.

Black Angel

My daughter Sunny worked in South Africa. Back home in Canada, I prayed every day for her safety. One day she and another girl went to an orphanage in a certain township. As the afternoon passed and evening set in, the girls watched desperately for the car that was to pick them up and drive them home to their apartment. Darkness fell and they faced the reality that their ride had "fallen through". The area they were in was definitely an unsafe place for two young girls to be walking alone.

Although it was likely they could be robbed or attacked, they decided to head out, the sooner the better. To make matters worse, as soon as they left the orphanage they noticed the street lights ahead of them were out.

Sunny, who considered herself "street wise", quickly became aware that there was someone behind them. When she glanced over her shoulder, she saw a big black man closely following them. He was carrying something under his arm. The girls did not sense any danger from him and comfortably forged ahead on the dark road. Two men approached out of the darkness. Sunny and her friend could hardly breathe but the men passed by without paying them any attention.

Relieved beyond words, the girls continued on. After about twenty minutes of brisk walking, they saw the street lights shining down on the road ahead. They were almost home.

The big black man behind them paused under the lights before turning off down a side street. He gave the girls a warm smile. They wondered who he was and where he came from. They did not doubt he had purposely escorted them to safety. Was he an angel? They did not know, but both girls realized the item he was carrying under his arm was a large Bible!

Footsteps in the Wall

Often when people go into an old abandoned house they say, "If only these walls could talk!" We can imagine the fascinating stories and events that may have taken place in there. The next story happened in this old house when people still lived in it.

The Sloan house near Fielding, Saskatchewan

The mantle clock chimed eleven. Roy and Herby glanced uneasily at the clock above the eerie shadows that were dancing in the lamplight. Their white haired father, Les, paid no attention as he dealt another round of cards. The three men looked tired yet they stayed up. Could it be that they were afraid to blow out the coal oil lamp and go to bed?

The bachelors' farm house was old and it needed a good cleaning. It had once been a bustling, crowded home filled with children and warmth, visitors, good food and fiddle music. But tonight memories of those bygone days had faded. Roy and Herby had not married and so they lived on at the farm with their tall, temperamental Irish father in the house where their mother had died.

Roy was a man of few words, always quiet and good at mechanics. Herby had become the cook when his sisters left home. His specialty was fried potatoes and onions and when he took a break in the kitchen he grabbed his guitar and sang a few country tunes. He was short and wide and he often joked that he was built more for "comfort than for speed".

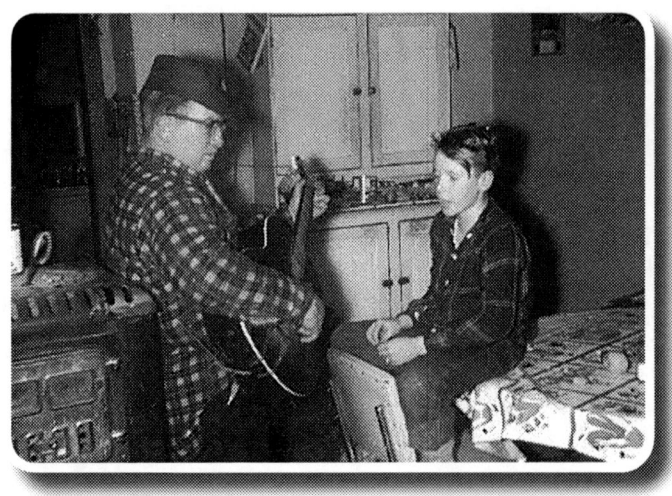

Herby playing his guitar, nephew Leroy singing

But there was no joking at the table as the hour grew late and the card players avoided going to bed. Then, they heard it— a bump inside the wall, then louder, then running sounds of little footsteps. Les threw his cards in the middle of the table. "Time for bed," he said gruffly, and blew out the light.

Night after night the noises continued -- sometimes loud, sometimes a rattly sound, and almost always, the patter of swiftly moving feet. To top it off, household items went missing. First, Roy growled that someone had stolen his cuff links. Les searched high and low for his shiny jackknife that he used to shave off pieces of chewing tobacco. In the kitchen Herby noticed that spoons were rapidly disappearing. What was going on in the night? Who'd want spoons anyway? One night when the moon was bright, Herby set four spoons out on the cupboard. In the morning, all of them had vanished.

They didn't talk about it but all through the winter months, night time fear gripped them. Some nights all was quiet. Other times the noises continued for a long time.

It was a moonlit night. Roy slept with a flashlight beside his pillow. Les lay awake staring at the ceiling while Herby braced himself when the banging started and prayed for morning. Suddenly, there was a thunderous sound, as if something had crashed in the living room of the house. Herby, Roy and Les, all leaped out of bed. They met each other in the hall, wide-eyed but determined to face their visitor.

A tall hat rack lay on the floor along with a plant it had taken down. Just for an instant they saw the disappearing tail of their intruder.

"A packrat!" Les said. "I haven't seen one of those since I was a kid!"

In the morning Les hired a man from town to come out and close off all the holes in the house that would have given entry to their unwelcome guest. The exterminator showed them a huge cache of shiny objects in the dirt cellar under the house.

There were spoons galore, Les's jackknife, marbles, even the large tin lid of a tobacco can! The packrat had been busy packing away treasures, running in the space between the walls. And of course, he was especially active on nights when the moon shone in the window, highlighting the shiny silver objects in the house.

Packrats are about 12 inches long. They are nocturnal and they love to find shiny objects and pack them away.

Ned Walker's Horses

My mother knew the people involved in this story and she believed it to be true. I also believe it happened but it is your choice to -- believe it, or not!

It happened about 100 years ago in what is called "the early days" on the Canadian prairies. People came from many countries of the world to follow their dream of owning land. The offer of $10 for 160 acres was irresistible.

The Walker family moved to Saskatchewan at that time. All of their children were grown up. Their youngest son, Ned, was not married and he lived with his parents. He was a very gentle young man and poor in health, but he was cheerful and especially kind to animals. His father was exactly the opposite, with a violent temper when any thing or anyone annoyed him. He was known to yell and curse at his farm animals.

Life in the new land was very hard. They managed to dig a well, put up fences, build a house and buy some cattle and horses. Ned had his own excellent team of horses. He had trained them well. They were evenly matched and although they were not particularly big horses, they were willing to do any work their owner asked them to.

There was land nearby where trees were available to any farmer who needed firewood. The only problem was that this land was swampy and hard to get to. Mr. Walker and Ned waited until the ground froze in winter and then cut down a lot of trees. They took some home on their sleigh pulled by their horses, and the rest was left for another day.

Ned was not feeling well that night and ended up in bed with pneumonia. As it turned out, Ned's other health problems had weakened his body. Before Christmas Ned was dead and his parents were broken-hearted.

Mr. Walker became even more angry and abusive. His hot temper was ready to boil over at any moment. His wife said he couldn't even get long with himself! It was a long, cold winter.

In April the sun shone down on the Walker farm and the snow began to melt. Mr. Walker was in need of firewood and remembered the trees he and Ned had left behind in the swamp. He decided to go get them while the ground was still frozen. He left before noon, driving Ned's team of blacks. The road into the swamp was soft; obviously winter was over and he had come just in time. The trees were still there in a large, neat pile awaiting pick-up. Fearing the trail would be too soft to return the next day, Mr. Walker loaded all the poles on the sleigh. It was a heavy load but this team of horses had never refused any challenge Ned had given them.

They started off well, but before they had gone a half mile, the sleigh runners sank deep into the ruts. The heavy load was impossible. As Mr. Walker yelled and urged the horses on, they lunged forward over and over, unable to budge the heavy load. He flew into a rage. He grabbed a nearby willow whip. He beat both horses over and over on their heads and their backs, yelling and swearing. This went on for some time as Mr. Walker vented his pent up anger.

Suddenly and quietly, a young man stepped out of the willows in the swamp. It was Ned. He took the whip from his father's hand and threw it far into the bush.

"Don't whip them anymore, Dad, they've had enough."

Silence fell on the scene. Ned disappeared. The poles were quickly unloaded. Ned's father gently led the horses forward on to solid ground a few feet ahead. From that moment on, William Walker was a changed man. His temper was gone. He never again cursed at any one or anything, and Ned's horses were the best cared for team in the country.

These beautiful little girls are Ned Walker's relatives.
One of them is named Beryl.

The Dying Chickens

Cousin Clipper wearing dark colored shirt

Summer was a 'crazy busy' time for my Mom. Besides her usual farm work which included milking cows, carrying water from the well, cooking, cleaning and looking after her many children, she tended a big garden and was hostess to a steady stream of visitors from the beginning of the summer to the end.

Raising chickens each summer made even more work for my Mom. The new chicks arrived by train from the hatchery.

The cheep-cheeping cardboard boxes they came in had holes along the sides so the little yellow balls of fluff could breathe. It was fun to peek in the holes before we got them home, to see a fuzzy gold carpet of chicks!

Life was easy for us when we were small kids on the farm. We had little chores like bringing in a few sticks of wood from the woodpile to the kitchen cook stove, but mostly we ran barefoot and played games like 'cowboys' and 'house'. We made a playhouse in the trees with boxes and old dishes. We practiced our balance by walking on the corral fences which gave us the courage to later walk on the high ridge of the barn.

We loved our kittens and had at least one of our very own each summer. Even our cousins from the city often got to claim a cat for the duration of their visit, and most of them were fascinated with life on the farm. Clipper was one of those cousins. He was mischievous and was always pulling jokes. Maybe the reason I didn't like him was because *I* liked to be the one making people laugh. Anyway, he and I fought with each other. I could hardly wait till it was time for him to go back to Vancouver Island where he came from.

As the summer progressed, the chickens wandered all over the yard, which was a bad combination with the fact that we kids went barefoot! Those white birds with black trim on their wings and necks were 'on the grow', nice and plump, and ever closer to becoming a tasty chicken dinner for the family.

On the way to the barn one morning, my Mom saw one of the biggest chickens lying dead on the grass. She examined it and couldn't see any reason it had died. No cuts, no evidence of being sick. The same afternoon she found a second lifeless mound of feathers in the yard. Another fine big chicken had 'bit the dust'. Mom called all the kids and asked what we knew about it. Nothing.

One by one the chickens were dying--in different places, here and there. This was an expensive problem and my mom was determined to solve it. She searched the yard for clues. She knew the murderer wasn't a coyote or the chickens would have been eaten up. My mom was a bit of a detective and she wasn't about to give up until she had put an end to the killing.

Behind the granary she found a puzzling contraption. There, almost hidden from view, was cloth bag, actually a ten pound sugar sack, tightly stuffed with old rags. A rope was tied to it. Could this be the weapon used to attack her chickens? My Mom had her suspicions.

We didn't know it, but from that moment on, but she was watching everything and every one of us like a hawk. That afternoon while Mom was taking big brown loaves of bread out of the oven, Cousin Clipper slipped outside through the screen door. Mom was not surprised to see him duck behind the granary. Before he could get speed up swinging his murder weapon in a circle, aiming at yet another chicken, my Mom grabbed his arm from behind.

"You young devil!" she yelled. "What are you trying to pull off?"

The reign of terror was over. Clipper's holiday at our farm ended soon after that. No one was happier to see him go than I was—unless, of course, it was the chickens!

A couple of survivors!

A Fur Coat in July

This event occurred many years ago, in the 1930's, when my Aunt Olive was a young woman. She was a Bible College student at the time, and she was a believer in the power of God and His protection.

On an exceptionally hot summer afternoon, Olive was shopping in downtown Vancouver, Canada. Have you ever had that strange sensation when you felt that someone is watching you? That's what Olive experienced as she walked along the crowded street. She looked up and froze with fear. An extremely tall woman was quickly approaching, her cold eyes fixed on Olive's face. As bizarre as it may seem, the woman was wearing a long fur coat—and on such a hot day! The woman's hands were outstretched towards Olive's throat. The others on the street appeared totally oblivious to what was happening. Olive gasped out a one word prayer: "Jesus!" Instantly, she found herself on the other side of the street, walking in the other direction. The woman in the fur coat was nowhere to be seen.

CHARLOTTE EVELYN SLOAN

Olive on her wedding day

A Plumeria Blossom

Do you know what a plumeria is? It is my friend Bonnie's favourite flower. She loves its delicate petals and its unique scent. Many years ago when she arrived in Hawaii, her husband Ron placed a plumeria lei around her neck.

Not long ago Ron died and Bonnie missed him every day, all day long. Ron's brother and his wife invited her to go to Mexico with them. She was trying to make the best of her new life alone.

Although she had no heart for it, she went. In Mexico, she felt even worse. One evening on her way to dinner, another couple joined them. Now there were *two* couples---five people altogether and Bonnie felt like a 'fifth wheel'.

As they walked down an outdoor stone stairway, a strange thing happened. A perfect plumeria blossom wafted down from above and landed at Bonnie's feet. Mary, the lady Bonnie had just met, exclaimed, "It's a plumeria! I thought plumeria blooms only in Hawaii!"

Bonnie was comforted. They did not stop to search out the source of the plumeria, but Bonnie pressed the blossom in a book. It is still a reminder to her, as it was on that evening in Mexico, of happier times with the one she loved.

Toddler in the Wheat Field

Animals are amazing. They will often protect and rescue a human who is lost or in danger. We don't understand how they know what to do, but they do.

The day my baby girl started to walk, she actually ran on her tiptoes! By the time she was two years old, she was still running. She had bouncy brown curls and I took so many cute pictures as she played with her brother and our black and white border collie named McDuff.

We lived on a farm with wheat fields all around the yard. On a warm summer afternoon, I suddenly realized my girl was gone. I checked inside the house and through the yard. Her four year old brother said sadly, "I don't see her." I couldn't see her either and I was worried. When I looked at the nearby fields, my heart sank. The grain was taller than she was. A toddler could be totally lost in there. It would be like the old saying, "trying to find a needle in a haystack". I was comforted when I noticed that McDuff was also missing.

The fields were big and I could hardly decide where to go first. Then…at that moment, a sight I will never forget! First a movement in the wheat; then emerged a little girl with brown curls! She had her hand on the dog's back. McDuff had found her in the field and brought her home!

CHARLOTTE EVELYN SLOAN

Here is the little girl the dog rescued.

Treasure in the Cellar

Jerry and his car

Many of the first pioneer houses did not have a real basement under them. There was just a hole in the ground under a part of the house which served as a handy storage area for potatoes and carrots, and maybe some canned fruit, vegetables, jam and pickles. Often unwelcome guests such as families of mice would burrow their way in, wanting to share the little house on the prairie. We had a skunk in our cellar, and one time a muskrat, but that would be another story.

This story is about a cellar that had something very different in it. Here and there, rusty wires were sticking out of the dirt walls. The men who found those wires were mystified and they were determined to figure it out.

Jerry was a bachelor all his life. Some people said he was too stingy with his money to get married. He had a motor bike which was quite a 'keen machine' in those days. And, he had a car that he was very proud of.

He also had a girlfriend named Esther for 24 years, but they never married. He lived in his house and Esther lived in hers, but she faithfully did his laundry and often cooked for him. She rode on his motorbike with him and they spent lots of time together. She hoped he would be willing to get married but apparently he didn't want to spend money on a wife.

After all those years, Jerry was still a bachelor when he died. He had saved all his money for himself. After he died, some people went to clean out his little house. When they went down the wooden ladder to the cellar, they took a lantern so they could see. That's when they made a fascinating discovery. First, someone spied a wire sticking out of one of the dirt walls. He didn't think much of it until he noticed another, and then another. The men began to dig out the first wire, making a little tunnel in the dirt. A couple of feet into the wall, they discovered that the wire was attached to a tin can. Imagine their surprise when they pulled out the can and looked inside. What do you think was in it? It was full of money!

They spent a long time that day digging out all those little brown wire ends. There were lots of them and before the day was over, they carefully searched the walls one more time to be sure they had found them all.

FOOTSTEPS IN THE WALLS AND OTHER MYSTERIES

There were even cans containing coins that Jerry had found in birthday cakes so many years before when he was a kid. Jerry was a man who loved his money-- all of it-- but it was the same for him as for everyone else in the end. As the old saying goes, "you can't take it with you when you go!"

Jerry, Esther and her sister Helen riding on behind!

Wait Here!

This story was told to me by my friend Alex. It is a story about his mother and the miracle of protection she was given as a young girl. Her family lived in Poland during World War II. Day after day, they heard about the enemy soldiers ruthlessly entering people's homes, plundering, beating the men and taking the women hostage.

Alex's mother was a beautiful teenage girl. She believed that God would protect her. One day she packed a few of her belongings because she sensed that it was time for her to go. As soon as it was dark, she went down the stairs and stepped out alone into the street. Suddenly, she felt an arm reach out and pull her into a small space between two buildings. A voice whispered, "Wait here! It's not safe."

Almost afraid to breathe, she pressed against the wall, listening to the clomp-clomp of the soldier's boots. They passed by without even looking towards her hiding place. She then heard them go up the stairs to the apartment from which she had just escaped.

After they passed, she realized there was no one beside her. She never knew who it was that pulled her in to safety and said, "Wait here!" Alex said his mother found her way to a safe place and was never once stopped or molested by her enemies. Even when she was old, she was unable to recount the story without tears.

Fog on the River

My sister Sharon, her husband Bob and I had stayed overnight at his parents' farm home. In the morning we drove down the winding road to the North Saskatchewan River, where we planned to cross the water on a small ferry. We would be in our town in plenty of time for Bob to start work at the bank and for me to be dropped off at my high school.

But--we had not planned on the fog. It was really socked in. I remember that the ferry man's was named Bud. He walked down the hill from his house to meet us. He shook his head. "We'll just have to wait till the fog burns off," he said.

We waited. We waited some more. We realized that if didn't get across the river soon, we would be late for work and school. All three of us were 'big' on prayer. We bowed our heads and one of us, I don't remember who, prayed out loud. "Dear God, you know we have to get across the river right away. Please clear off the fog."

Every trace of the fog did not suddenly vanish as we had hoped it would. Instead, a path cleared in front of us. We could now see the ferry at the edge of the water. The fog moved back a little further on each side, until there was a wide space right across the water.

Bud spoke to Bob through the car window. He seemed perplexed. "I guess I can take you across." We drove on to the ferry. We felt like the Israelites in the Bible story of the Red Sea piling up on the sides and providing a clear pathway through.

It was eerie and awesome to see that fog, still as thick as ever, on either side of us. As soon as we reached the other side of the river, we quickly drove off the ferry and up the road to our town. As we looked back down at the water, the fog instantly rolled back into the space through which we had crossed. Bud and his ferry were stuck on our side of the river until the fog would later burn off in the morning sun.

That happened many long years ago, but I still remember how the fog looked and how we felt as we witnessed that memorable answer to our prayers.

It was an open ferry, something like this one.

When Lassie Hid the Pups

A farmer sat down for breakfast and said to his wife, "Today I'll have to shoot Lassie's pups. I asked everybody I saw in town yesterday and nobody seems to want one."

"That's a shame," his wife answered. "They're the best looking batch she's ever had."

"I know," the farmer answered, "but we can't have a bunch of adult dogs around the farm. One dog alone is by far the best."

Just then Lassie left her spot under the table and whined at the door. The wife opened the door so the dog could go outside. Later, she threw some scraps of food outside but didn't see Lassie or the pups. She thought nothing of it as they often played down by the barn throughout the day. In the evening when they called Lassie to go get the cows, she didn't come. It was the first time in all the years they had her, that the farmer had to go get the cows on his own. It took a long time to find them without her help.

"I've looked everywhere," the man said the next day. "There's neither a hide nor hair of any dog to be seen on this farm." A week passed, and then another. They gave up on ever seeing her again. The farmer was talking about trying to buy a new dog. Two more weeks passed.

Imagine the surprise for the farmer and his wife when one morning, a very thin mother dog and her six big and beautiful pups came up out of the pasture! The farmer shook his head in disbelief.

"Whatever it takes, I'll find a home for every one of them!" he told his wife. Lassie seemed to understand. She knew she had saved her pups!

Farm dogs are smart. This one is helping carry wood
to the house to burn in the kitchen stove.

Who Said That?

An eight year old boy stayed home from school because he had the flu. His mom felt sorry for him and fixed up a special chair, pillows and a blanket for him in the kitchen. As she did her morning work, the boy quietly rested in the chair.

Suddenly, he turned his head and his eyes were wide. "Who said that?" he asked.

His mom knelt down beside him. "Who said what?"

"Someone called my name. Who was it?"

His mom told him she had not heard anything. The boy was confused. "But someone called my name. I know I heard it. It said *Kevin*."

She asked him what the voice was like, and he had an interesting way of describing it. "It was a nice voice; it was a voice like *I love you*."

His mother then told him that perhaps it was God who called his name. She told him a story from the Bible.

A little boy named Samuel who was awakened in the night by a voice calling his name. He ran to the next room and asked Eli the priest what he wanted. It happened twice and both times Eli said, "It was not me who called you. Go back to bed." The third time, Eli told the little boy, "If you hear someone call your name again, it will be the voice of God. Say, these words: Speak Lord for your servant hears you." Sure enough, that is what Samuel did and God had a special message for him.

Kevin grew to be a man and sometimes when he is sad or has serious difficulties, he remembers that day in the kitchen when he was eight years old, and Someone called his name!

(I know this really happened because I am the Mom in the story and Kevin is my son.)

Take Me Home!

Katrina was a grey and white mama cat who had babies every year and chased mice like crazy. One time I borrowed her for a couple of weeks because there were mice in my basement and she was a great hunter. My sister Shelley and her friend Verna slept on the floor upstairs because they were scared of the mice down below. In the middle of the night Katrina proudly put a dead mouse on Verna's pillow! My brother borrowed that same cat for his classroom as he was a teacher and wanted to teach his students about farm animals having babies. She had a batch of kittens in a box under a student's desk and you can imagine how the pupils loved having all those cats in the classroom!

Well, then my sister Trudy moved into an older house and unfortunately, some mice had already moved in before she did.

There were lots of them. Time to borrow Katrina one more time! She had a good reputation of clearing out mice-- just give her a day or two and she would chase and kill and scare them right out of the house! This time something went wrong, Katrina was very unsettled. She wasn't interested in catching mice. She let them run wherever they wanted. She meowed and stood at the door and went from room to room. It was most annoying and the mice were laughing at her. My sister was fed up having a cat around who was no good to her. Finally, after a couple of days, this wonderful cat who always behaved well wherever she went, sneaked into Trudy's bedroom. Pretty soon Trudy smelled something horrible. She couldn't find the cat but there was a huge, stinking cat mess in the middle of her bed!

"That does it! Back to the farm you go!" So they put Katrina in a box and drove thirty miles to her home, complaining all the way about that stupid cat. But there was something going on that Trudy didn't know about. Katrina had something else on her mind.

When they got to the farm and let her out of the box that cat took off like a shot towards the barn. They were baffled.

They followed Katrina to the barn and guess what they found? A batch of tiny, mewing newborn kittens starving for their mother's milk!

They must have been born just before Trudy took her to the city but no one knew her secret. No wonder that mother cat had had no interest in catching mice. She was longing to get back to her kittens before it was too late. In the only way she knew how, by misbehaving so badly, she was begging my sister, "Take me home!"

Cats are tough. Those hungry little kittens survived, and grew into good mousers like their mother, Katrina!

High and Lifted Up

I stayed with my Mom and Dad for a few weeks when they lived in the town of Maymont which is a few miles north of the river.. Early one morning Mom called me outside. "Chuck, come and take a look at this!"

I ran out into the fresh morning air to see what she had to show me. She pointed south and what I saw totally amazed me. Usually, we could see nothing in that direction except some houses and the flat gravel road going out of town. Mom and I stood there gazing at the strangest sight you can imagine. There was some mist in the distance but through it, above the road, we could clearly see the North Saskatchewan River and the hills beyond the river banks. I had never seen anything like it and told my Mom I couldn't believe my eyes. I remember what she said. "It's the river, and it's high and lifted up."

What we saw is called a 'mirage'. I can't explain how a mirage works but it is a phenomenon in nature that has often startled people the world over.

My Mom and Dad, Evelyn and Ted Sloan

A Wet Night on the Highway

When I was a kid a farm dog was more than a pet. He was a working member of the family, ever ready to bark if someone came into the yard or if a coyote was after the chickens. He also rounded up cattle and pigs and watched out for the safety of the kids.

Our neighbours had a good dog named King. He was very fluffy and pretty with a white fur collar all the way around his neck. One day King went missing. They called and called but he didn't come. They got in their truck and drove around to ask the neighbours if they had seen him. They looked in the ditches to see if he had been hit and killed by car, but he had vanished. As the old saying goes, 'not a hide or hair of him could be seen!"

We went to the fair one summer day with those same neighbours. By now King had been gone for several months. We were driving home after dark and several of us kids were crowded into the back seat of their car. Cars didn't have any seat belts in those days so we sat on each other's lap to make more room. The wind came up and it started to rain. As we drove along to the tune of the windshield wipers, Gug, the driver suddenly noticed an animal on the side of the road. He slowed down the car and asked his wife.

"Did you see that? It looked a bit like King!"

She answered, "I thought the very same thing!" Gug got the car stopped and stepped out in the rain to check it out.

Suddenly, a ball of fur came rocketing down the road towards us. We opened the back door to get a better look and he jumped right in on top of us. Have you ever smelled a wet, dirty dog? It is an awful smell but we didn't care! No mistake - it was King! We were all so excited we couldn't quit patting his head and talking about it.

What a strange thing to happen! There are still many unanswered questions. Where had King been all those months? Had someone stolen him? Our neighbours were thrilled to have him back on the farm but they never found out the secret of where he had been and why he was there on that highway so many miles from their home just at the perfect time when his family was driving by in the rain.

Jim and Wayne are wearing plaid shirts in this picture.
Imagine how happy they were when their
dog, King, leaped into the car.

Donkey Come Home

Daylin and his little friend, Brook

What is your favourite animal? My favourite is the elephant. My second favourite is a donkey, especially a miniature donkey because they are the sweetest animals on earth.

My last story is about a man who loved his donkeys and mules. He much preferred them to horses. Many years ago people depended mostly on horses for farm work and transportation. As time went on, most people in that community sold their horses and bought new cars instead. Old John Johnson thought they were crazy! "You can have your fancy cars and trucks," he said. "I'm sticking with my donkeys and mules!"

On wet, rainy days John Johnson hitched up his fastest team of black mules and headed for town. Just as he had hoped, cars and trucks were always stuck deep in the mud on the road along the way to town. Instead of pulling them out with his team, John Johnson just laughed loud and long as his mules trotted past the mired down cars.

By and by the old man could no longer do the work on his farm. He had to move to a home for old people. His farm and all the animals were sold at an auction. People came for miles around to the sale. Most of them had never owned either mules or donkeys and they were curious. The auctioneer called out, "How much am I bid for this team of black mules, the fastest in the country?" The sale went on all afternoon. Finally at the end of the day, the last donkey was sold. Old John's belongings and his animals were paid for and taken to various faraway farms.

New owners moved into the farmhouse.

The new owners put in new fences, took down the old hitching post and fixed up the yard. Many, many years passed by. One Sunday morning they looked out the kitchen window to see a strange and unexpected visitor coming down their lane. They saw a very old, thin donkey plodding along, slowly placing one foot ahead of the other. He looked straight ahead and kept walking till he got to the very spot where the old hitching post had been. There he stopped, his head hanging low. Home at last! From some farm somewhere, this old donkey had traveled on his own until he found his way home.

Farewell Note

Remember at the beginning of this book I told you there is a hidden picture in the cover photograph? In case you haven't found it, here's what to look for. It is the perfect head of a duck.

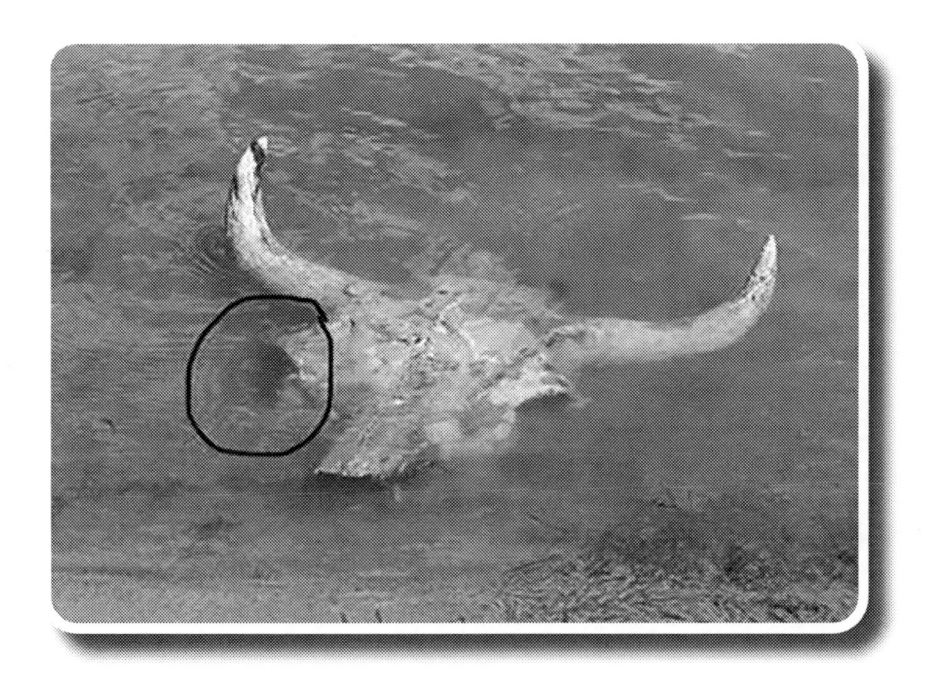

I'll bet you have some interesting mystery stories of your own. Here are some blank pages for you to add to this book.